A M E R I C A N
MOTORCYCLE
C L A S S I C S

**BY DOUG MITCHEL AND
THE AUTO EDITORS OF CONSUMER GUIDE®**

Publications International, Ltd.

Louis Weber, C.E.O.
Publications International, Ltd.
7373 North Cicero Avenue
Lincolnwood, Illinois 60646

ISBN 0-7853-0668-4

Photo Credits:

David Gooley—12-13, 58-59

Buck Lovell—6-7, 8-9, 30-31, 44-45, 46-47, 66-67, 74-75, 76-77

Vince Manocchi—48-49

Doug Mitchel—cover, 4-5, 10-11, 14-15, 16-17, 18-19, 20-21, 22-23, 24-25, 26-27, 28-29, 32-33, 34-35, 36-37, 38-39, 40-41, 42-43, 50-51, 52-53, 54-55, 56-57, 60-61, 62-63, 64-65, 67, 68-69, 70-71, 72-73, 78-79, 80-81, 82-83, 84-85, 86-87, 88-89, 90-91, 92-93, 94-95

Special thanks to:

My family and friends.

Pete & Joey Bollenbach, Rich Crouthers, Chris Hajer, Rich Jagodzinski, Jim & Nella Kersting, Dave Kiesow, Buck Lovell, Lee Mattes, Steve Rowe, Brian Vegter, John Vodden, Dale Walksler, and Buzz Walneck.

CONTENTS

FOREWORD

It is generally accepted that the first motorcycle was constructed in 1885—one year before the first car. A mobile monstrosity few would have dared ride, it was the work of Gottlieb Daimler and Paul Maybach of Germany, colleagues of Nikolaus Otto (after whom the four-stroke Otto cycle is named).

Though subsequent efforts on both sides of the Atlantic were essentially bicycles with small motors attached, that first motorcycle looked little like the pedal-powered transports of the day. A heavy wooden frame suspended the engine low between knee-high wheels; the front wheel was steered by a tiller. The rider sat atop a thin leather saddle propped up over the backbone of the frame, and two small "training wheels" kept the rig from tipping over.

With a displacement of only 270 cubic centimeters (roughly 16 cubic inches), the crude engine managed to wheeze out about ½ horsepower at 800 rpm. Even that, however, is quite astounding considering its primitive design. To feed fuel to the engine, air was passed over a bowl of gasoline and admitted to the cylinder via an atmospheric intake valve (meaning that it was opened by cylinder vacuum rather than by a mechanical valve train). The mixture was ignited by a platinum tube heated at its external end by a gas flame, with the resulting burned gases exiting through a pushrod-operated exhaust valve.

More efficient fuel metering and increasingly reliable ignitions greatly advanced the state of the art, and shortly after the turn of the century, carburetors and magnetos helped motorcycles become accepted forms of transportation. As one might expect, competitive events soon followed; the winners boasting of their triumphs in advertising, the losers going back to the drawing board to improve upon their designs.

It is estimated that, in the early part of the century, there were hundreds of motorcycle manufacturers in the United States alone. Most were backyard builders using engines supplied by De Dion of France, Minerva of Belgium, or others, strapped on to a frame of their own choosing. But the Depression and two world wars weeded out most of these entrepreneurs, and at the end of World War II, only Harley-Davidson and Indian returned as major manufacturers—and the latter wouldn't last long afterward.

But from the beginning, the American motorcycle industry produced some fascinating machines. While European manufacturers typically leaned toward lighter, smaller-displacement bikes better suited to their congested cities and limited thoroughfares, U.S. makers took the "bigger is better" approach, building heavy, powerful cruisers that thundered down our open highways. Though some notable light and middleweight motorcycles were produced, it is the big-inch heavyweights that characterized the American motorcycle industry the world over.

American Motorcycle Classics takes you on a nostalgic trip through the history of these fascinating pieces of Americana. We hope you enjoy the ride.

1896 MARKS

More bicycle than motorcycle, the Marks was built in San Francisco, California, before the turn of the century. Pedals were used to start the engine, scale inclines, and generally act as a backup to the temperamental engine. Since the carburetor concept was in its infancy and not yet universally adopted at this time, the single-cylinder 15-cubic-inch engine used an evaporative-wick system that metered fuel with "by-guess-and-by-gosh" accuracy.

Despite its primitive nature, the Marks incorporated some rather modern concepts, such as a twist-grip throttle and even a rudimentary front suspension. Tensioned leather-belt drive was common for the era, as was the rear bicycle-type coaster brake. But since the engine had no internal lubrication system, the rider had to carry a can of oil and monitor the engine's needs to prevent piston seizure or other mechanical malady.

With a top speed of perhaps 15 mph (downhill with a tail wind), one wonders why any rider would put up with the finicky engine and constant oiling ritual when there were perfectly good horses around. No doubt many at the time felt the same way.

Year:	1896
Manufacturer:	Marks
Model:	—
Engine Type:	Single-cylinder De Dion
Displacement:	15 cubic inches
Valve Train:	Atmospheric intake, mechanical exhaust
Carburetion:	Evaporative wick
Transmission:	Single-speed
Front Suspension:	Leading link with extension springs
Front Brake(s):	None
Rear Suspension:	Rigid
Rear Brake:	Coaster
Weight:	Approx. 100 pounds
Final Drive:	Leather belt
Owner:	Stan Dishong

Opposite page: *Box mounted above the rear wheel holds a dry-cell battery that provides energy for the ignition system. Fumes from the evaporative-wick system entered the engine through the nickel-plated "carburetor" at the base of the cylinder.* This page, top right: *Leather drive belt was kept under proper tension by a spring-loaded pulley.* Left: *The atmospheric intake valve was sucked open by cylinder vacuum, closed by cylinder pressure. The exhaust valve, hidden inside the black finned casting ahead of the cylinder, functioned in the normal manner.* Above: *Leading-link forks stretched a pair of door springs to absorb shocks.*

1903 INDIAN

Shortly after the turn of the century, a Mr. Carl Hedstrom mounted a single-cylinder De Dion engine onto a tandem bicycle for the purpose of pacing then-popular bicycle races. George Hendee, a bicycle manufacturer from Springfield, Massachusetts, saw the contraption and suggested to Hedstrom that the two of them pool their knowledge and resources to produce motorbicycles commercially. Hedstrom agreed, and the Indian Motorcycle Company was born. Only two or three machines were built in 1902, but their success in local speed trials, hill climbs, and endurance races did not go unnoticed, and the next year saw production rise to 143.

Most pre-1910 motorcycles look as though the manufacturer simply bolted a motor and its accessories onto a common bicycle—which indeed was usually the case. But the 1903 Indian used its engine as a stressed frame member, effectively replacing the downtube beneath the seat. As with most motorcycles of the era, suspension was nonexistent (save for the spring-mounted seat), and pedals were used to start the engine. However, Indian used a direct-drive chain rather than a tensioned leather belt to turn the rear wheel.

While most production Indians mounted their gas tank behind the seat, the Indian shown is thought to be a prototype or racing machine, as the tank is mounted beneath the upper frame tube. The 13-cubic-inch De Dion engine produces about 1.75 horsepower, enough to propel the Indian to a breathtaking 25 mph.

Year:	1903
Manufacturer:	Indian
Model:	—
Engine Type:	Single-cylinder De Dion
Displacement:	13 cubic inches
Valve Train:	Atmospheric intake/ mechanical exhaust
Carburetion:	Improved Hedstrom
Transmission:	Single-speed
Front Suspension:	Rigid
Front Brake(s):	None
Rear Suspension:	Rigid
Rear Brake:	Coaster
Weight:	Approx. 98 pounds
Final Drive:	Chain
Owner:	Stan Dishong

Far left: *The Indian relied upon a simple bicycle-type coaster brake to haul it down from speed. Above: Ignition timing was controlled by rotating the "d" shaped casting on the right. The De Dion-designed engine was built for Hedstrom and Hendee under license. Left: A relatively new invention at that time, the spark plug replaced primitive "hot tube" ignition, providing more control over the timing of the combustion process.*

1913 INDIAN 61 TWIN

Indian's 1913 model year was one of choices and changes. Prospective buyers of a 61 Twin were offered several mechanical improvements, as well as their pick of transmissions and suspension systems.

Riders were given a more comfortable motorcycle with the adoption of a new "Cradle Spring Frame" that incorporated the world's first swingarm rear suspension system—though it was somewhat different in design to what we commonly see today. When the rear wheel encountered a bump, two vertical rods actuated a pair of leaf springs attached to the frame beneath the seat. This joined a conventional (at least for Indian) trailing-link front fork that worked on a similar principle. For those suspicious of the new technology, a rigid frame remained available. Braking was still accomplished with an internal shoe/external band rear brake, which incidentally conformed to Britain's "dual brake" requirement, though it might not have been exactly what the Brits had in mind.

Also still in use was the F-head (overhead intake, side-valve exhaust) V-twin engine claimed to produce a rousing seven horsepower. Indian offered singles as well, but the V-twin accounted for 90 percent of the company's production. Standard models offered but a single speed, though a two-speed transmission was available as an option.

Year:	1913
Manufacturer:	Indian
Model:	61 Twin
Engine Type:	V-twin
Displacement:	61 cubic inches
Valve Train:	Overhead intake, side exhaust
Carburetion:	Hedstrom
Transmission:	Single-speed (two-speed optional)
Front Suspension:	Leaf spring
Front Brake(s):	None
Rear Suspension:	Swingarm with leaf springs (rigid available)
Rear Brake:	Internal shoe/external band
Weight:	NA
Final Drive:	Chain
Owner:	Dale Walksler Collection

Left: *Valvetrains for both the overhead intakes and side exhausts ran* au naturel, *without any form of cover to protect them from the elements.* Above: *Swingarm rear suspension was a pioneering concept for the day. Unlike modern designs, however, the Indian's swingarm pushed a pair of rods against two leaf springs bolted to the frame beneath the saddle. Front suspension worked on the same principle.*

1914 EXCELSIOR C-4

In its day, Excelsior was a big name in motorcycling, often ranking just behind Indian and Harley-Davidson in popularity. Based in Chicago from 1908 to 1931, it was a division of the Schwinn Bicycle Company, which is still in existence today. Although it produced some small two-strokes, Excelsior was better known for its four-stroke 30-cubic-inch singles, V-twins of 45 and 61 cubic inches, and later an "adopted" inline four. All of the four-stroke models used F-head engines.

For 1914, this 30-cubic-inch C-4 single ("4" designating four horsepower) gained chain drive to replace the previous belt. Its single-speed transmission drives through a multi-disc clutch that is controlled by twisting the left hand grip. The trailing-link front suspension incorporates a leaf spring—essentially the same arrangement used by Indian. A spring-loaded saddle post compensates for the rigid rear frame, and only the rear wheel is fitted with a brake.

Excelsior purchased Henderson in 1917, adding that company's famous inline-four motorcycle to its offerings. William Henderson was asked to stay on, but soon left to form Ace (see entry), where he built a machine very similar to the original design that bore his name.

Though Excelsiors sold fairly well through the years, Schwinn discontinued the marque in 1931 to concentrate on its bicycle business.

It should be noted that at least two other companies, both based in Europe, have marketed motorcycles under the Excelsior name. An English manufacturer produced a variety of models starting before the turn of the century until the mid-Sixties, and a line of German Excelsiors was built between 1901 and 1939. Aside from sharing the same name however, none had any association with the others.

Year:	1914
Manufacturer:	Excelsior
Model:	C-4
Engine Type:	Single-cylinder
Displacement:	30 cubic inches
Valve Train:	Overhead intake, side exhaust
Carburetion:	Schebler
Transmission:	Single-speed
Front Suspension:	Trailing link with leaf spring
Front Brake(s):	None
Rear Suspension:	Rigid
Rear Brake:	External band
Weight:	Approx. 265 pounds
Final Drive:	Chain
Owner:	Warwick Eastwood

Far left: *Evident on the fork neck was Excelsior's connection with the Schwinn Bicycle Company. Throttle and clutch were controlled by rotating the handgrips, the motion being transferred by intricate jointed shafts rather than cables.* Left: *Right side of engine shows exposed valvetrain and engine-turned crankcase. Small lever at the top of the crankcase is for the compression release, also actuated by a jointed shaft.* Above: *Lever on the side of the fuel tank controls the ignition advance through—you guessed it—a jointed shaft.*

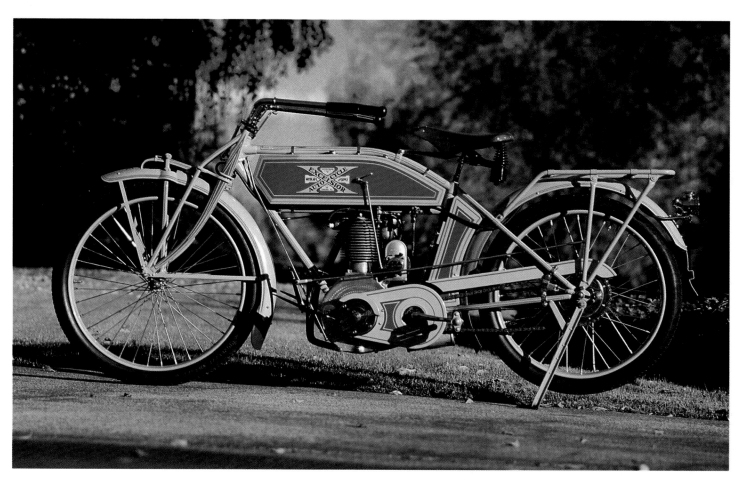

1914 HARLEY-DAVIDSON MODEL 10C

Harley-Davidson built its first motorcycle in 1903, little more than a bicycle with a single-cylinder three-horsepower engine mounted within the frame tubes. The first of the famed V-twins appeared in 1909, but the bulk of Harley sales remained the single-cylinder machines. These grew in sophistication, and in 1913, Harley-Davidson introduced the 5-35, which stood for five horsepower from 35 cubic inches. Previous Harleys were belt-driven; the 5-35 offered the option of chain drive, which was much more positive in operation.

Further improvements—and a few choices—came with the 1914 models. Three versions of the 35-cubic-inch single were offered: The base 10A model with single-speed belt drive; the 10B, which substituted a chain for the belt; and the 10C (pictured) that added a new two-speed rear hub.

There were other refinements as well. The exhaust-valve springs were enclosed to protect them from the elements, connecting rods were fitted with roller bearings, and a "step starter" helped ease starting and reduce back-firing. Floorboards made their debut in 1914 and were packaged with two more advancements. A foot pedal joined the traditional hand lever for activating the clutch, allowing the rider a choice of which to use. Brakes could likewise be applied either by the new forward-mounted brake pedal or by back-pedaling on the pedals as before.

Other aspects of the Model 10s were not as advanced. Braking was done by a sole band-type rear brake, front suspension took the form of a leading-link fork activating coil springs (which proved only marginally effective), and the sprung saddle was the only form of "rear" suspension.

Year:	1914
Manufacturer:	Harley-Davidson
Model:	10C
Engine Type:	Single-cylinder
Displacement:	35 cubic inches
Valve Train:	Overhead intake, side exhaust
Carburetion:	Schebler
Transmission:	Two-speed rear hub
Front Suspension:	Leading link with coil springs
Front Brake(s):	None
Rear Suspension:	Rigid
Rear Brake:	Internal band
Weight:	NA
Final Drive:	Chain
Owner:	Dale Walksler Collection

Top: Clutch could be activated either by a hand lever or foot pedal, both mounted on the left side of the bike. Left: Tank-mounted speedometer with odometer and trip odometer was gear-driven off the rear wheel. Above: Rod with circular end underneath the sprung seat actuates the exhaust cut-out.

1915 HARLEY-DAVIDSON 11F

In the Teens, technology was advancing rapidly at Harley-Davidson. The company's 61-cubic-inch F-head V-twin engine, while not a true overhead valve design (only the intake was ohv), was more advanced than the common flathead engines sported by most competitors. Furthermore, the 1915 models gained an automatic oiler and larger intake valves, the latter helping to boost output to 11 horsepower. That rating, by the way, was guaranteed by Harley-Davidson, the only motorcycle manufacturer to back their quoted power claims in writing.

Another new feature for 1915 was an electric lighting system supported by a magneto generator and a vacuum battery cut-off. A neat feature of this design was that the taillight could be removed for use as a nighttime service light. (The model shown is equipped with a Prest-O-Lite headlight, which is gas-powered.)

Elsewhere, the 11F was perhaps not so advanced. Front suspension was by leading-link fork with coil springs, but it didn't provide much comfort, allowing only slightly more wheel travel than the nonexistent rear suspension. The expanding-band rear brake now featured double action to increase braking efficiency, but it wasn't what could be called state-of-the-art, and starting was still accomplished by pedaling the engine up to speed.

Year:	1915
Manufacturer:	Harley-Davidson
Model:	11F
Engine Type:	V-twin
Displacement:	61 cubic inches
Valve Train:	Overhead intake, side exhaust
Carburetion:	Schebler
Transmission:	Three-speed, hand shift
Front Suspension:	Leading link with coil springs
Front Brake(s):	None
Rear Suspension:	Rigid
Rear Brake:	Internal expanding band
Weight:	325 pounds
Final Drive:	Chain
Owner:	Bob Maxant

Far left: Harley's famous V-twin debuted in 1909, and by 1915 it produced a guaranteed 11 horsepower. An automatic oiling system was new that year, but it was still of "total loss" design—that is, after the oil had run through the engine, it was simply deposited on the ground. Left: Shift pattern placed first gear towards the front of the bike, with neutral between first and second. Clutch could be operated either by a foot pedal or the chrome hand lever sprouting from below the seat. Above: Gas-powered Prest-O-Lite headlamp was a popular accessory.

1917 HARLEY-DAVIDSON MODEL F

For the 1917 model year, Harley-Davidson made several line-wide changes. A switch from the earlier gray and red paint scheme to Military Olive and red was likely prompted by the escalating war in Europe. Indeed, after the U.S. entered the war in April of 1917, half of Harley's production went overseas.

This 1917 5-35 sports the typical suspension of the era—such as it was. The front forks provide two inches of wheel travel; there is no rear suspension, and the spring-mounted saddle provides little additional comfort. Sidecar riders fared a bit better. The elaborate wicker body rests on a tubular steel frame, supported in the rear by a large leaf spring.

As before, the 5-35 designation stood for five horsepower from 35 cubic inches. That's not much power from a fairly modern engine, but the lone rear coaster brake probably didn't inspire the confidence to travel any faster than five horsepower would take you.

Year:	1917
Manufacturer:	Harley-Davidson
Model:	F
Engine Type:	Single-cylinder
Displacement:	35 cubic inches
Valve Train:	Overhead intake, side exhaust
Carburetion:	Schebler
Transmission:	Three-speed, hand shift
Front Suspension:	Leading link with coil springs
Front Brake(s):	None
Rear Suspension:	Rigid
Rear Brake:	Coaster
Weight:	NA
Final Drive:	Chain
Owner:	Pete Bollenbach

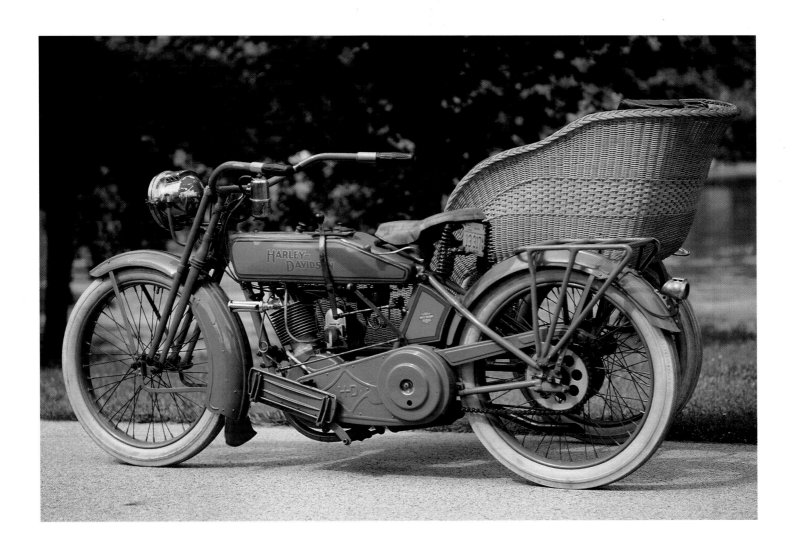

Above: *Spring-mounted saddle made up for the lack of rear suspension—sort of. Curved lever under the seat actuates a chrome exhaust whistle (left) mounted to the top of the cylinder, which was a "cool" accessory of the day. Vertical gold-colored lever shifted gears in the three-speed transmission; the angled lever activated the clutch, which could also be controlled with a foot pedal.*

1918 POPE L-18

Pope Manufacturing Company had been building Pope-Tribune automobiles and Columbia bicycles for years before they joined the two and began producing motorcycles in 1908. Early models were singles, but a V-twin followed in 1912, and by 1918, Pope was known for quality construction and innovative engineering. This 61-cubic-inch V-twin illustrates the point well. It featured overhead valves at a time when most competitors offered flathead or F-head engines. Crankcases were cast from an aluminum alloy, and each set of pistons and connecting rods were matched with another pair of the exact weight. Its "Armored Magneto" ignition allowed use in all types of weather, and each motorcycle was road-tested before being shipped.

Front suspension consisted of a trailing link actuating a leaf spring. But perhaps the most intriguing aspect of this Pope is the rear suspension. Not only was having *any* rear suspension unusual at that time, but the design was uniquely Pope. Unlike the common swingarm that is used on motorcycles today, Pope mounted the rear axle in a carrier with posts that moved up and down in sleeves mounted to the frame, extending a pair of springs on impact. Wheel travel was minimal, but something was better than nothing and this became a major selling feature.

Unfortunately, this 1918 Pope represents the last of the line. With World War I raging in Europe, Pope suspended motorcycle production later that year to concentrate on building machine guns, and after the war, only the bicycle portion of the business was revived.

Year:	1918
Manufacturer:	Pope
Model:	L-18
Engine Type:	V-twin
Displacement:	61 cubic inches
Valve Train:	Overhead valves
Carburetion:	Schebler
Transmission:	Single-speed
Front Suspension:	Trailing link, leaf spring
Front Brake(s):	None
Rear Suspension:	Axle carrier on vertical rods, coil springs
Rear Brake:	External band
Weight:	NA
Final Drive:	Chain
Owner:	Pete Bollenbach

Far left: *The Pope's clutch could be actuated either by a hand lever or a foot pedal.* Left: *The company was known for its quality and innovation, evident in such items as the unusual rear suspension design. The rear axle was mounted in a carrier with two posts that moved up and down inside sleeves mounted to the frame. Springs were secured to the posts at the top and to the frame at the bottom, so they stretched when the wheel hit a bump.* Above: *Overhead-valve engine was another unusual feature at that time.*

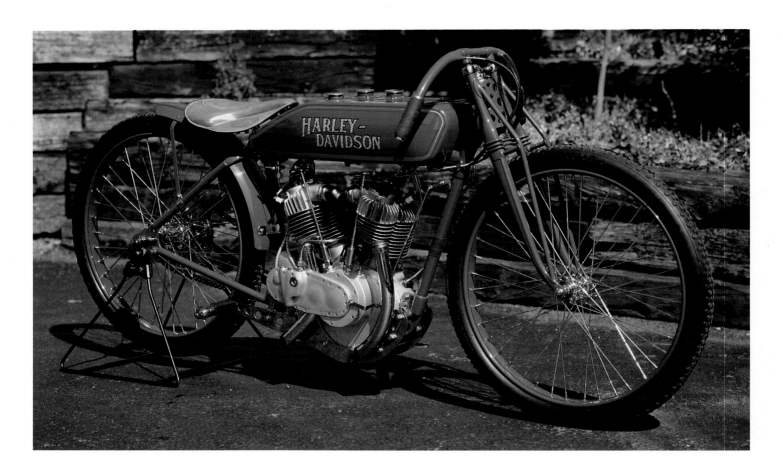

1922 HARLEY-DAVIDSON JD RACER

Early motorcycle races were as much a test of durability as of speed, since many events were so grueling that only a handful of entries would finish the race in any kind of reasonable time. Just making it to the finish line in one piece was often considered a victory in itself.

In 1908, Walter Davidson himself entered—and won—the Long Island Endurance Run. But other than the occasional endurance or mileage competition, Harley-Davidson showed little official interest in racing—though they did tout the victories of independent riders who won on Harleys.

But that philosophy began to change as Pope, Indian, and other rivals began sending out factory-backed teams. Harley-Davidson followed suit in 1913, and though their early efforts were less than successful, management was convinced they could win, and their machines improved rapidly.

By the late Teens, the company had become the dominant force in racing. In 1921, a Harley-Davidson motorcycle won every championship, most at the hands of the company's stable of riders known as the "Wrecking Crew." Soon afterward, Harley dropped its racing effort, as management decided to quit while the company was on top.

This 1922 JD Boardtrack Racer was built at the peak of Harley's racing success. For these high-speed boardtrack events, brakes were considered superfluous and suspension nearly so, as the Merkel-style front fork provided only about one inch of travel. The F-head V-twin displaced 61 cubic inches, putting the JD into the popular 1000cc class.

Year:	1922
Manufacturer:	Harley-Davidson
Model:	JD Boardtrack Racer
Engine Type:	V-twin
Displacement:	61 cubic inches
Valve Train:	Overhead intake, side exhaust
Carburetion:	Schebler
Transmission:	Single-speed
Front Suspension:	Merkel-style with coil spring
Front Brake(s):	None
Rear Suspension:	Rigid
Rear Brake:	None
Weight:	NA
Final Drive:	Chain
Owner:	Dale Walksler Collection

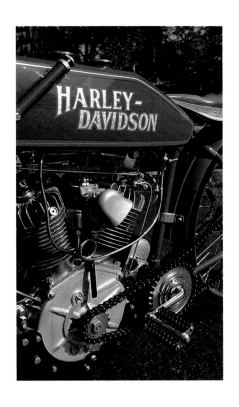

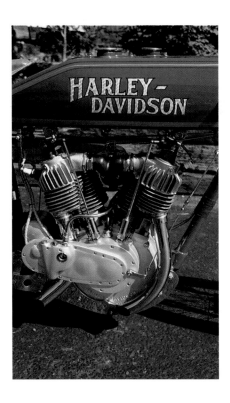

Opposite page: *Merkel-style front fork moved up and down (though not much), compressing a coil spring within the frame neck.* This page, far left: *Pedals were used to start the engine, and the small hand pump mounted to the side of the fuel tank was used to feed oil to the engine.* Left: *Like roadgoing Harleys, the racers used F-head V-twins of 61 cubic inches; unlike their street counterparts, however, they had a single-speed transmission and no brakes.* Above: *Creature comforts were minimal; riders probably felt lucky to get this padded-leather saddle.*

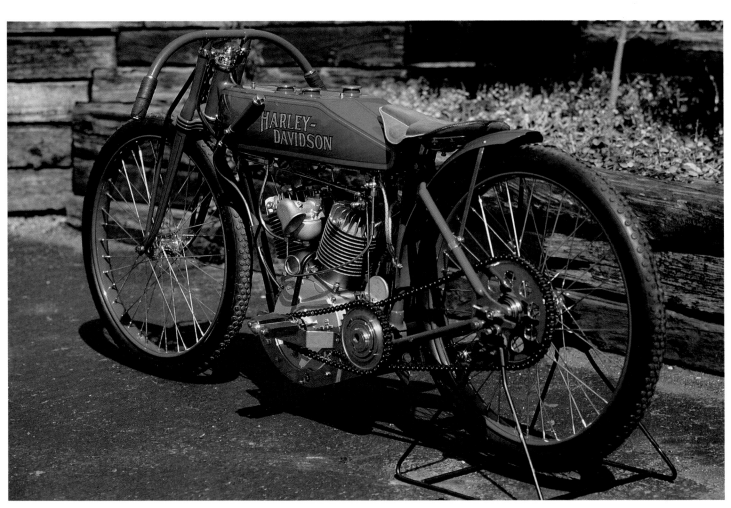

1924 HARLEY-DAVIDSON FHAC RACER

There have been many forms of motorcycle competition over the years, but few were as exciting and dangerous as boardtrack racing.

As the name implies, the surface was made from 4-inch-wide wooden slats, and most tracks had corners with banking up to 60 degrees without a straightaway in sight. On these "soup bowls," top riders were able to run at speeds of over 100 miles per hour—this on a bike with *no brakes*. Consequently, one of the most challenging tracks on the circuit was the Chicago Boardtrack, which was long and flat, its corners showing only a hint of banking.

These lightweight racers were specially built with a single-speed transmission, simple front suspension, and an engine with such high compression that a tow car was usually required to get them started. An ignition cut-out switch allowed some engine braking, but this was hardly a substitute for a good set of binders.

This 1924 FHAC Boardtrack Racer represents a mere handful of racing machines built by Harley-Davidson after 1922. It differs from the 1922 JD primarily in front suspension design: The JD has a Merkel-style front end, where the whole fork moves up to compress a coil spring in the frame neck; the FHAC uses a more conventional leading-link with coil springs. Only established riders were allowed to buy a machine of this type, and very few were ever assembled.

Year:	1924
Manufacturer:	Harley-Davidson
Model:	FHAC Boardtrack Racer
Engine Type:	V-twin
Displacement:	61 cubic inches
Valve Train:	Overhead intake, side exhaust
Carburetion:	Schebler
Transmission:	Single-speed
Front Suspension:	Leading link with coil springs
Front Brake(s):	None
Rear Suspension:	Rigid
Rear Brake:	None
Weight:	NA
Final Drive:	Chain
Owner:	Dale Walksler Collection

Far left: *Racers used a high-performance version of Harley's 61-cubic-inch F-head V-twin. Compression was so high that riders often could not start the bikes by pedaling the engine up to speed—they had to be push-started by a car.* Left: *As opposed to the Merkel-style front end found on earlier racers, the FHAC used leading-link "castle" forks.* Below: *Look Ma, no brakes!*

1925 HARLEY-DAVIDSON JD

Though primitive by today's standards, the 1925 Harley-Davidson JD featured the latest in technical advances and boasted increased levels of riding comfort. The redesigned frame was lower and wider than before, and the frame fittings were now made of stronger drop-forged steel. JDs were advertised as being ideal for use with a sidecar, and the frame was engineered with that purpose in mind. Weight increased by 25 pounds, but the new design resulted in a three-inch-lower seat height. Since frames still lacked rear suspension, riders appreciated the softer fork springs and new contoured saddle, the latter of which also offered six-position height adjustment.

While a few JDs left the factory with clear headlight lenses, most were fitted with a diffuser lens that allowed for better light dispersion. The shift lever was moved farther forward along the side of the tank for convenience, and a fork-mounted tool kit made a debut appearance.

Year:	1925
Manufacturer:	Harley-Davidson
Model:	JD
Engine Type:	V-twin
Displacement:	74 cubic inches
Valve Train:	Overhead intake, side exhaust
Carburetion:	Schebler
Transmission:	Three-speed, hand shift
Front suspension:	Leading link with coil springs
Front Brake(s):	None
Rear Suspension:	Rigid
Rear Brake:	External band
Weight:	405 pounds
Final Drive:	Chain
Owner:	Jim Kersting Family Collection

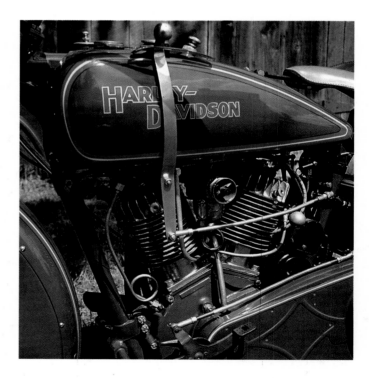

Left: Reliefs were formed into the fuel tank to accommodate the overhead intake valve and its exposed valvetrain. Polished tubes running from the crankcase into the base of the cylinders house the valvetrain for the side exhaust valves. External-band rear brake is applied with an automotive-style foot pedal. Above: Tall shift lever controls the three-speed transmission, while the foot pedal flips back and forth to engage/disengage the clutch.

1926 INDIAN PRINCE

Indian's fortunes rose and fell during the Roaring Twenties, but when this Prince was built in 1926, the company was on a high. Intended as an entry-level vehicle, the Prince was promoted on the slogan "You can learn to ride it in five minutes." Of course, Indian hoped that those lured into motorcycling by the amiable Prince would return to buy a larger, more expensive Chief, or perhaps the soon-to-be-released inline-four model.

With its 21-cubic-inch flathead single and managable 265-pound curb weight, the Prince made an ideal first motorcycle. Like most others of the period, it had a spring-mounted seat to make up for the lack of rear suspension. In front, girder-style forks compressed a coil spring to provide a nominal amount of suspension travel. Also common for the era was the three-speed transmission and single drum brake fitted to the rear wheel.

A number of improvements marked the 1926 edition of the Prince. Most noticable was the European-inspired rounded fuel tank that replaced the wedge-shaped tank used earlier. A redesigned saddle lowered the seat height a few inches, and handlebars were lengthened to reduce the long reach to the grips.

Year:	1926
Manufacturer:	Indian
Model:	Prince
Engine Type:	Single-cylinder
Displacement:	21.25 cubic inches
Valve Train:	Side valves
Carburetion:	Schebler
Transmission:	Three-speed, hand shift
Front Suspension:	Girder fork with coil spring
Front Brake(s):	None
Rear Suspension:	Rigid
Rear Brake:	Drum
Weight:	265 pounds
Final Drive:	Chain
Owner:	Pete Bollenbach

Far left: *Chrome shift rod is "conveniently located" below and inside the rider's right knee. Vertical rod extending above fuel tank is for the compression release.* Left: *Early kickstarter had exposed teeth— watch those pant legs.* Above: *Schebler carburetors have been used on generations of American motorcycles.*

1926 ACE

When William Henderson ran into financial trouble in 1917, his Henderson Motorcycle Company was purchased by Excelsior, the motorcycle arm of the Schwinn Bicycle Company. William and several other key personnel were to carry on to supervise the production of Henderson's popular four-cylinder motorcycle, but disagreements erupted and William left to form Ace. With new financial backing, William produced another four-cylinder motorcycle similar to the Henderson, though no parts were compatible.

Ace produced a great motorcycle but proved to be a short-lived proposition, suffering several financial setbacks before finally being purchased by Indian in 1927. Indian continued to offer what was essentially the Ace four—wearing Indian logos of course—until World War II.

The Ace was powered by an inline four displacing 77 cubic inches. An Ace/Schebler carburetor fed fuel to the air-cooled cylinders, and a Splitdorf magneto supplied the spark. Power was transferred through a foot-operated multi-disc wet clutch to a three-speed transmission with hand shift. The leading-link front fork compressed a single coil spring mounted inside the frame neck, but the rear wheel was solid-mounted.

Weighing in at about 395 pounds, the Ace wasn't particularly light, but proved to be both powerful and durable. Several transcontinental records were set on virtual stock machines piloted by such famous riders as Cannonball Baker and Wells Bennet. The fact that this motorcycle continued in production for over two decades with little more than suspension and brake updates is further testimony to its enduring design.

Year:	1926
Manufacturer:	Ace
Model:	—
Engine Type:	Inline four
Displacement:	77 cubic inches
Valve Train:	Overhead intake, side exhaust
Carburetion:	Ace/Schebler
Transmission:	Three-speed, hand shift
Front Suspension:	Leading link with cartridge-type coil spring
Front Brake(s):	None
Rear Suspension:	Rigid
Rear Brake:	Dual drums
Weight:	395 pounds
Final Drive:	Chain
Owner:	Richard Morris

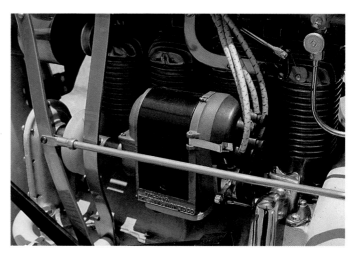

Left: *A speedometer (which is driven off a separate sprocket on the rear wheel) and ammeter dominate the top of the fuel tank. The forward lever is the gearshift; the rearward lever operates one of two rear drum brakes. A foot pedal operates the other rear brake. Above: Splitdorf magneto provided spark to the 77-cubic-inch inline four.*

1930 INDIAN FACTORY HILLCLIMBER

Hillclimbing had reached the peak of its popularity in the late Twenties, as almost anyone could participate in the sport due to its low-tech requirements. To be truly competitive, however, one needed some specialized equipment.

The Indian Hillclimber pictured here was just such a machine. One of only four built by the factory in 1930, it carried a 45-cubic-inch V-twin equipped with overhead-valve cylinder heads (Indian's production V-twins were flatheads) and 14:1 compression. Running on alcohol, it transferred a thundering 58 horsepower to the single-speed transmission.

Also specialized was the lightweight rigid frame sporting a conventional (for Indian) trailing-link fork with leaf spring. Braking was provided by a rather small rear drum—stopping not being a big concern in a hillclimb—and the huge rear tire was usually fitted with chains for added traction. A pressurized fuel tank kept the juice flowing as the "slant artist" did his thing, the exposed valve train furiously pumping away beneath him.

Year:	1930
Manufacturer:	Indian
Model:	Hillclimber
Engine Type:	V-twin
Displacement:	45 cubic inches
Valve Train:	Overhead valves
Carburetion:	Linkert
Transmission:	Single-speed
Front Suspension:	Trailing link with leaf spring
Front Brake(s):	None
Rear Suspension:	Rigid
Rear Brake:	Drum
Weight:	NA
Final Drive:	Chain
Owner:	Dale Walksler Collection

Above: Indian built only four of these special hillclimbing machines in 1930, this one apparently for "Slim" Nelson. Left: Special overhead-valve cylinder heads graced the 45-cubic-inch V-twin engine. (Other Indian V-twins were flatheads.) Knob on top of fuel tank pumps in air to pressurize the tank, aiding fuel flow at extreme angles.

1935 INDIAN CHIEF

Despite being demoted to second fiddle by the 1927 debut of the Ace-based four-cylinder model, the V-twin Chief made up the bulk of Indian sales in the prewar market. The 74-cubic-inch Chief competed directly with the large Harley-Davidsons of the time, though many thought the Indian, with its flowing teardrop tank, to be the more graceful-looking of the two.

However, the big Chief was anything but graceful in slow-paced manuevers. Its suspension design, long wheelbase, and 480-pound curb weight conspired to make it feel clumsy around town, but once up to speed, these same features provided exceptional stability.

The buyer of a 1935 Chief was faced with a wide variety of options. Color choices were *reduced* that year to 13, though an extra $5 would buy any hue DuPont offered. Even the fuel and oil tanks were available in three different trim variations. An optional "Y" engine featured aluminum cylinder heads, heavy-duty valve springs, and a modified muffler. A four-speed transmission could be ordered to replace the standard three-speed.

New to the '35 version were redesigned fenders with larger valances to smooth out the styling, and a rebound spring for the ungainly front leaf suspension that helped smooth out the ride somewhat. Chiefs still lacked any form of rear suspension, though they did offer a spring-loaded seat post.

Year:	1935
Manufacturer:	Indian
Model:	Chief
Engine Type:	V-twin
Displacement:	73.63 cubic inches
Valve Train:	Side valves
Carburetion:	Schebler
Transmission:	Three-speed, hand shift
Front Suspension:	Trailing link, leaf spring
Front Brake(s):	Drum
Rear Suspension:	Rigid
Rear Brake:	Drum
Weight:	480 pounds
Final Drive:	Four-row chain
Owner:	Pete Bollenbach

Top right: *In its early years, the Chief's gear lever was found far back on the right, connected directly to the three-speed transmission.* Right: *Speedometers were mounted rather ungraciously on the top of the tank.* Far right: *When the front wheel encountered a bump, the trailing-link suspension would pull down on the leaf spring.*

1936 HARLEY-DAVIDSON EL

Compared to the rampant speculation that preceded it, the official introduction of the 1936 EL was a bit anticlimactic. Dealers got the facts at their annual convention in December of 1935, and though not as wild as the rumors had predicted, the 61-cubic-inch EL nevertheless set new standards for Harley-Davidson—not to mention the rest of the industry.

Most important was the switch from the old F-head design to overhead valves. Due to the resulting shape of the new rocker covers, the engine was dubbed "Knucklehead" by the motoring press, a nickname it is still fondly known by today. Equally significant was the new recirculating oiling system that eliminated the messiness and inconvenience of the previous "total loss" setup.

Unique to the 1936 EL are the rocker-shaft covers and air intake. The timing case cover was changed three times during the model year, each design a bit smoother than the last. Fuel tanks were welded and much sleeker than earlier examples, and the tank-mounted instrument cluster started a styling trend that would be followed for years to come.

Only about 1600 ELs were built in 1936 out of a total production of around 9800. Though volume was initially modest, the EL would go on to become one of the most popular models Harley-Davidson ever offered.

Year:	1936
Manufacturer:	Harley-Davidson
Model:	EL
Engine Type:	V-twin
Displacement:	61 cubic inches
Valve Train:	Overhead valves
Carburetion:	Schebler
Transmission:	Four-speed, hand shift
Front Suspension:	Leading link with coil springs
Front Brake(s):	Drum
Rear Suspension:	Rigid
Rear Brake:	Drum
Weight:	515 pounds
Final Drive:	Chain
Owner:	"Wheels Through Time" museum

Left: Harley's famous "Knucklehead" V-twin debuted in 1936, which got its nickname from the shape of its rocker covers. It featured overhead intake and exhaust valves; previous V-twins had overhead intakes and side exhausts. Also featured was a recirculating oiling system to replace the "total loss" system used before. Above: The EL was also the first Harley to get a tank-mounted speedometer, a styling element still in use today.

1937 HARLEY-DAVIDSON EL POLICE MODEL

Only one year after its debut, the EL was already undergoing some changes. Oil circulation on the 61-cubic-inch overhead-valve V-twin was improved by providing additional flow, and the bike's frame tubes were made of heavier-gauge steel with added reinforcements.

Featured here is a 1937 EL originally used by the California Highway Patrol (C.H.P.). By this time, Harley-Davidson had earned an enviable reputation for durability, evidenced by their widespread use in municipalities across the country. C.H.P. had ordered their first batch of Harleys, a fleet of JD models, in 1929.

The '37 EL made impressions elsewhere as well. In March of that year, Joe Petrali took a streamlined version to Daytona Beach and set a new American speed record of 136.183 mph. Joe Ham broke the 24-hour distance record, formerly held by a Henderson Four, by logging 1825.2 miles in a single day.

Year:	1937
Manufacturer:	Harley-Davidson
Model:	EL Police Model
Engine Type:	V-twin
Displacement:	61 cubic inches
Valve Train:	Overhead valves
Carburetion:	Schebler
Transmission:	Four-speed, hand shift
Front Suspension:	Leading link with coil springs
Front Brake(s):	Drum
Rear Suspension:	Rigid
Rear Brake:	Drum
Weight:	NA
Final Drive:	Chain
Owner:	"Wheels Through Time" museum

Far left: *Though only in its second year, the "Knucklehead" V-twin got an improved lubrication system for 1937. Other features shown on this police model include new instrument-panel graphics (above), along with a redesigned taillight and a running light on the front fender (below).*

1939 HARLEY-DAVIDSON EL

For 1939, the 61-cubic-inch "Knucklehead" powered EL was the recipient of several mechanical and aesthetic changes.

Heavy-duty valve springs were fitted to prevent valve bottoming, and a constant-mesh sliding-gear transmission helped reduce noise during shifts. The latter feature would last but one year and prompted a change in the shift pattern, placing Neutral between second and third gear.

Appearance was modified with new fuel-tank graphics and revised fender trim, while a color-matched instrument panel with "cats eyes" indicator lamps graced the top of the fuel tank. A new taillight aided visibility, and the oil tank was redesigned for the sixth (and final) time.

"Run what you brung" racing classes continued to be quite popular during this period, and the EL made for a competitive mount. Perform a few simple modifications, such as bobbing the rear fender, removing excess trim, upgrading the brakes, and lowering the handlebars, and the EL was ready to hit the dirt.

Year:	1939
Manufacturer:	Harley-Davidson
Model:	EL
Engine Type:	V-twin
Displacement:	61 cubic inches
Valve Train:	Overhead valves
Carburetion:	Schebler
Transmission:	Four-speed with hand shift
Front Suspension:	Leading link with coil springs
Front Brake(s):	Drum
Rear Suspension:	Rigid
Rear Brake:	Drum
Weight:	NA
Final Drive:	Chain
Owner:	Dale Walksler Collection

Above: *Revised tank graphics and fender trim are shown on this 1939 EL.* Left: *Already known for its power and reliability, the "Knucklehead" engine continued to be refined, gaining stronger valve springs inside and a new air cleaner outside.* Below: *Instrument panels were restyled with body-colored housing, "cats eyes" indicator lamps, and simple black-on-white speedometer face.*

1940 INDIAN 440

Indian began offering inline fours after acquiring Ace in 1927, and the first examples were little more than Aces with red paint and Indian logos on their tanks. The unusual engine had overhead intake valves and side exhaust valves, a configuration known as an F-head.

This four-cylinder model remained virtually unchanged until 1936, when the valve layout was reversed in an effort to wring more power from the 77-cubic-inch engine. Often referred to as the "upside-down" Indian, the new model was a dismal failure. Maintenance was more difficult than before and overheating became a problem, so Indian reverted to the original design two years later.

The 1940 version, called the 440, adopted skirted fenders that added a more streamlined look. They also added about 36 pounds to the already imposing mass, now totaling 568 pounds. But the 440 boasted not only the typical Indian leaf-spring front suspension but also an atypical plunger-type coil-spring rear suspension, and if anything, the added weight made it ride smoother than ever.

Year:	1940
Manufacturer:	Indian
Model:	440
Engine Type:	Inline four
Displacement:	77 cubic inches
Valve Train:	Overhead intake, side exhaust
Carburetion:	Schebler
Transmission:	Three-speed, hand shift
Front Suspension:	Trailing link with leaf spring
Front Brake(s):	Drum
Rear Suspension:	Plunger-type with coil spring
Rear Brake:	Drum
Weight:	568 pounds
Final Drive:	Chain
Owner:	Pete Bollenbach

Left: *Indian's inline four was originally used in the Ace, a '20s motorcycle designed by William Henderson. When the four-cylinder model was discontinued in 1942, the engine was virtually the same as it had been twenty years earlier. Above: Instrumentation included a speedometer and ammeter mounted in a chrome housing.*

1940 CROCKER BIG TANK

When the subject of prewar American V-twins comes up, Harley-Davidson and Indian are undeniably the most popular makes. But in terms of performance, neither could hold a candle to a Crocker.

While the original Crockers were single-cylinder speedway machines, the first production models were large-displacement V-twins. Manufactured in Los Angeles, California, from 1936 to 1940, only 61 Big Twins were built, making the survivors very rare indeed.

Contrary to some rumors, the Crocker used no Indian or Harley-Davidson components. Albert Crocker had enough experience to design and produce most of the parts at the company's Los Angeles location. Since Crockers were built to special order, engine displacement was whatever the customer wanted. (The model shown has an 80-cubic-inch engine, but some had up to 100.) However, all Big Twin production engines had overhead valves; early models had a hemispherical head with exposed valve springs, while later models had a flat squish-type combustion chamber with enclosed valve springs. Most were magneto-fired, with carburetors by Linkert or Schebler. All came with a nearly indestructible three-speed transmission, the housing for which was cast into the frame.

Two different Big Twins were offered, a Big Tank model and a Small Tank version, both fuel tanks being made of cast aluminum. The latter could be easily identified by the two mounting bolts that ran all the way through the tank halves. It also had a more upright fork angle that shortened the wheelbase and quickened the steering, making it better suited to racing.

On the street, at least, Crockers were formidable machines, able to humble most other bikes of the era. But due to their small numbers, few riders ever saw one—which is probably just as well, considering the humiliation that could follow.

Year:	1940
Manufacturer:	Crocker
Model:	Big Tank
Engine Type:	V-twin
Displacement:	80 cubic inches (up to 100 cubic inches available)
Valve Train:	Overhead valves
Carburetion:	Linkert or Schebler
Transmission:	Three-speed, hand shift
Front Suspension:	Girder fork with coil springs
Front Brake(s):	Drum
Rear Suspension:	Rigid
Rear Brake:	Drum
Weight:	Under 500 pounds
Final Drive:	Chain
Owner:	Richard Morris

Crockers were fast, beautifully finished, and very rare. Big Twin
engines were made to order, so a customer could dictate
specifications, but all were overhead-valve V-twins. Early versions
(above) *had exposed valvetrains; later models* (left) *had the
valvetrains enclosed.*

1941 INDIAN 741

World War II prompted both Indian and Harley-Davidson, the only major surviving manufacturers, to increase military motorcycle production tremendously. Indian's primary contribution, the 741, was used mainly by couriers and scouts. With its detuned flathead V-twin displacing only 30.5 cubic inches, the 450-pound 741 provided lackluster performance but impressive durability.

Though based on Indian's prewar Thirty-fifty (for 30.50 cubic inches), a lightweight V-twin model, the 741 was fitted with a stronger Sport Scout (45 cubic inch) transmission. It also used a 1.25-inch-longer girder fork to increase ground clearance, and added a large oil-bath air cleaner that could be cleaned or replaced quickly in the field. Military contract specifications required certain other modifications, such as blackout lights, machine-gun scabbard, and heavy-duty luggage rack.

A hand-shifted three-speed transmission and foot-operated clutch were standard, both being the norm for the day. It must have been confusing for servicemen to go from an Indian to a Harley, however, because the Indian's clutch disengaged when the lever was pushed down with the toe and engaged when it was pushed down with the heel. Harleys were just the opposite.

Following the war, a number of 741s were sold in the civilian market as military surplus. And many of today's restored Indian Thirty-fiftys and Scouts are fitted with at least a few military spare parts.

Year:	1941
Manufacturer:	Indian
Model:	741
Engine Type:	V-twin
Displacement:	30.5 cubic inches
Valve Train:	Side valve
Carburetion:	Linkert
Transmission:	Three-speed, hand shift
Front Suspension:	Girder fork with coil springs
Front Brake(s):	Drum
Rear Suspension:	Rigid
Rear Brake:	Drum
Weight:	450 pounds
Final Drive:	Chain
Owner:	Bob Stark

Like the Model T, the 741 came in any color the customer wanted—and Uncle Sam wanted Olive Drab. Above: Military specifications dictated the fork-mounted carriers, rear luggage rack, and oversized air cleaner. Left: Speedometer looks to have been added as an afterthought. Note the small blackout light on the front fender. Below: Power was supplied by a 30.5-cubic-inch V-twin based on the prewar Thirty-fifty engine.

1942 HARLEY-DAVIDSON XA

Though not the most beautiful motorcycle Harley-Davidson ever built, the XA is certainly one of the rarest and most unusual. Born of a government contract and intended for use by the Allies in the deserts of North Africa, only 1000 XAs were built—all in the first half of 1942.

Even an avid enthusiast could be forgiven for not recognizing the XA as a Harley-Davidson. For one thing, it has a 45-cubic-inch horizontally-opposed two-cylinder side-valve engine, the first (and last) time the Milwaukee company would ever attempt a horizontal "flat twin" layout (though a longitudinal flat twin was produced in the early Twenties). Based on a design used by BMW, it was probably thought to provide better engine cooling, an important factor considering its mission. Likewise the switch to shaft drive (also never used before or since) due to the devastating effect of sand on chains and sprockets. Other XA oddities included separate hand- and foot-operated shift linkages and solid 15-inch wheels.

Ironically, the XA never saw action overseas. Harley's more conventional WLA model was being produced concurrently with the XA and proved much more popular, with tens of thousands seeing service during the war. Another vehicle called the Jeep also entered the picture, and was chosen as the primary mode of transport for U.S. troops.

Year:	1942
Manufacturer:	Harley-Davidson
Model:	XA
Engine Type:	Horizontally-opposed twin
Displacement:	45 cubic inches
Valve Train:	Side valves
Carburetion:	L & L Mfg.
Transmission:	Four-speed, both hand and foot shift
Front Suspension:	Leading link with coil springs; single shock
Front Brake(s):	Drum
Rear Suspension:	Plunger-type with coil springs
Rear Brake:	Drum
Weight:	NA
Final Drive:	Shaft
Owner:	Jim Kersting Family Collection

Opposite page: *Typical Harley leading-link fork gained a shock absorber mounted on the right side.* This page, top row: *Speedometer was located in its normal position on the tank, and blackout lights were added to the fenders.* Below: *Horizontally-opposed flathead twin was connected to a four-speed foot-shift transmission and drove the rear wheel through a drive shaft—all very un-Harley-like.*

1942 INDIAN SPORT SCOUT

Introduced in 1920, the first Scout carried a 37-cubic-inch V-twin and was attended by the slogan "You can't wear out an Indian Scout." Time would prove that tag line quite appropriate. Though a larger 45-cubic-inch version was added in 1927, the original Scout was dropped after 1931 to be replaced by what was essentially the larger Chief fitted with the 45-cubic-inch engine—still carrying the Scout name. To satisfy those who missed the lighter, more nimble Scout of old, a 37-cubic-inch V-twin was mated to a smaller frame and called the Scout Pony. A 45-cubic-inch version was added in 1933, but neither one matched the standards of the original.

In 1934, a Sport Scout was introduced with the 45-cubic-inch V-twin in a small frame with girder front fork. As the name implied, this was Indian's "sports" model, intended to be the spiritual successor to the original Scout. It eventually evolved into the bike shown here.

Looking much like Indian's bigger 74-cubic-inch Chief, this 1942 Sport Scout still carried the 45-cubic-inch version of the flathead V-twin. It shared a plunger-type rear suspension with its bigger brother, but retained the girder forks in place of the Chief's leaf-spring front suspension, though the Chief would switch to a similar girder design after the war.

This 1942 model represents just a handful of civilian Scouts produced that year, as Indian was concentrating on military production. With the skirted fenders that appeared in 1940 and the plunger rear suspension adopted the following year, Scouts now tipped the scales at 500 pounds (Chiefs weighed in at about 560). As a result, Scouts were none too quick by this time, but provided style and comfort at a lower cost than the Chief.

Nonetheless, the Chief remained the big seller in the line, and Scout V-twins weren't built after the war, save for 50 special Daytona Sport Scout racers. The Scout name, however, would later be revived on a lightweight vertical twin.

Year:	1942
Manufacturer:	Indian
Model:	Sport Scout
Engine Type:	V-twin
Displacement:	45 cubic inches
Valve Train:	Side valves
Carburetion:	NA
Transmission:	Three-speed, hand shift; four-speed optional
Front Suspension:	Girder fork with coil springs
Front Brake(s):	Drum
Rear Suspension:	Plunger-type with coil springs
Rear Brake:	Drum
Weight:	500 pounds
Final Drive:	Chain
Owner:	Gerard J. De Persio

Far left: *Chrome instrument panel housed a speedometer and ammeter.* Left: *Like the Chief, Scouts carried this nifty Indian-head shift knob.* Above: *Despite its height, the plunger-type rear suspension provided only about 1½ inches of travel—though that was 1½ inches more than was offered by any Harley of the period.*

1946 INDIAN CHIEF

When Indian resumed production after the war, only one model was offered: the now-legendary V-twin Chief. Though a radical shaft-drive, 45-cubic-inch transverse V-twin had been designed for the U.S. military, only about a thousand were built and it wasn't sold as a civilian model afterwards. Its girder-style coil-spring front forks, however, were adapted to the new Chiefs, providing a full five inches of wheel travel versus the meager two inches allowed by the previous leaf-spring design. Though the rear still featured the same plunger-type suspension, the spring rates were softened. These changes resulted in an even smoother ride than before, a notable selling feature of the postwar models.

These Chiefs were otherwise the same as previous versions. The engine remained a 74-cubic-inch flathead V-twin and tank graphics were unchanged. As always, "Indian Red" was a popular color choice, though others—including two-tones—were available.

Year:	1946
Manufacturer:	Indian
Model:	Chief
Engine Type:	V-twin
Displacement:	73.62 cubic inches
Valve Train:	Side valves
Carburetion:	NA
Transmission:	Three-speed, hand shift
Front Suspension:	Girder fork with coil springs
Front Brake(s):	Drum
Rear Suspension:	Plunger-type with coil springs
Rear Brake:	Drum
Weight:	550 pounds
Final Drive:	Four-row chain
Owner:	Pete Bollenbach

Above: *Locking toolbox and rear crash bar were popular accessories of the day.* Left and below: *Another accessory was this spring-mounted sidecar, first offered in 1940, which carried fancy chrome speedlines and trim.*

1948 HARLEY-DAVIDSON FL

Changes came thick and fast in the postwar years at Harley-Davidson. A little 125cc two-stroke machine was introduced in 1948, the same year the company opened a 260,000-square-foot engine production facility in Wauwatosa, Wisconsin, a few miles west of the Milwaukee facility. But that year's biggest news—at least to collectors—came in the form of Harley's new FL model with its "Panhead" V-twin.

Replacing both the 61-cubic-inch overhead-valve Knucklehead and the 74-cubic-inch flathead V-twins, the overhead-valve Panhead was available in the same two displacements and incorporated several improvements. Beneath its roasting-pan-shaped rocker covers (from which it got its nickname) lay aluminum heads that were lighter and provided better cooling than their cast-iron predecessors. Hydraulic lifters reduced valve noise and eliminated most adjustments, while an improved oil circulation system resulted in longer engine life.

There were other changes as well. More chrome trim pieces gave the bikes a fancier look, and a steering-head lock was added in case the extra flash attracted the wrong kind of attention. A latex-filled saddle was available, as were eight equipment packages that let buyers tailor an FL to their own tastes. And Azure Blue, as seen on this example, was a new color choice.

Apparently these changes were appreciated by the motorcycling public, for Harley-Davidson sold a record 31,163 units in 1948. But even more big news lay on the horizon.

Year:	1948
Manufacturer:	Harley-Davidson
Model:	FL
Engine Type:	V-twin
Displacement:	74 cubic inches
Valve Train:	Overhead valves
Carburetion:	Schebler
Transmission:	Four-speed, hand shift
Front Suspension:	Leading link with coil springs
Front Brake(s):	Drum
Rear Suspension:	Rigid
Rear Brake:	Drum
Weight:	560 pounds
Final Drive:	Chain
Owner:	Dale Walksler Collection

Left: *The 74-cubic-inch flathead and beloved 61-cubic-inch "Knucklehead" V-twins were replaced by the "Panhead" engines in 1948, which fitted aluminum heads and hydraulic lifters under roasting-pan-shaped rocker covers. Both 61- and 74-cubic-inch versions were initially offered.* Above: *Instrument panels were dressed up in chrome and carried revised graphics.*

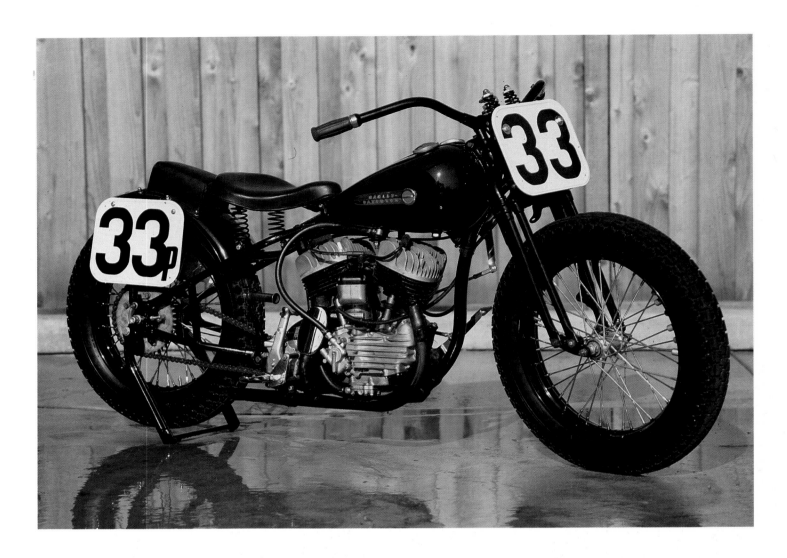

1948 HARLEY-DAVIDSON WR

Harley-Davidson began its factory racing effort in 1913. That's not to say Harleys weren't raced prior to that time—they were, and did quite well— but they weren't campaigned by factory-backed teams. Harley's involvement proved to be an on-and-off affair even before World War II temporarily halted all racing activity; but after the war, Harley-Davidson hit the race tracks with a vengeance.

One of the fruits of this effort was the WR, a 45-cubic-inch machine aimed squarely at C-class competition. While C-class was intended as a "run-what-you-brung" exercise for street bikes, WRs were stripped-down, purpose-built racers devoid of such "frivolities" as lights and brakes.

WRs used a rigid frame (no rear suspension) and a leading-link fork with coil springs. The engine was a low-compression flathead V-twin with 40 horsepower—and a very wide torque band. Since changing gears was still accomplished with a foot clutch and hand shifter, the engine's broad power curve required minimal shifting and proved quite effective on dirt ovals across the country. Overall, Harley won 19 of 23 National Championship races in 1948, and, probably not coincidentally, sold a record 31,000-plus motorcycles.

Year:	1948
Manufacturer:	Harley-Davidson
Model:	WR
Engine Type:	V-twin
Displacement:	45 cubic inches
Valve Train:	Side valves
Carburetion:	NA
Transmission:	Close-ratio three-speed, hand shift
Front Suspension:	Leading link with coil springs
Front Brake(s):	None
Rear Suspension:	Rigid
Rear Brake:	None
Weight:	NA
Final Drive:	Chain
Owner:	Dave Kiesow

WRs were serious racing machines (brakes were considered superfluous) that tore up the tracks in the late '40s and on through the '50s. The V-twin's wide power band minimized the number of throws necessary on the hand-shifted three-speed transmission. Left: Note that unlike early Harleys, first gear was back toward the rider.

1949 INDIAN ARROW

Indian's first postwar verticals, the single-cylinder Arrow and the Scout twin, arrived during the summer of 1948 as 1949 models. These smaller, cheaper machines were intended to draw a new crowd of riders into the Indian fold. The company apparently felt this project important enough that the production of the venerable Chief was temporarily suspended during 1949 in order to concentrate on this new breed of Indian.

The "entry-level" Arrow sported a 13.3-cubic-inch overhead-valve single-cylinder engine. Contrary to Indian custom, the clutch was hand-operated, the gearshift foot-operated. Modern hydraulic forks were fitted in front, and though the rear wheel was mounted to a rigid frame, customers could special-order their Arrow with the "plunger" rear suspension offered on larger Indians.

One point in the Arrow's favor was that it didn't look small and cheap, but rather like a lightweight racing bike. And light it was; at 245 pounds, it weighed less than half as much as the V-twin Chief. But a racer it wasn't.

Despite its attributes, the Arrow was short-lived. Some leftover '49s were sold as 1950 models, but the larger twin overshadowed the Arrow, spelling the end for this jaunty little single.

Year:	1949
Manufacturer:	Indian
Model:	Arrow
Engine Type:	Single-cylinder
Displacement:	13.3 cubic inches
Valve Train:	Overhead valves
Carburetion:	L & M Mfg.
Transmission:	Four-speed, foot shift
Front Suspension:	Hydraulic
Front Brake(s):	Drum
Rear Suspension:	Rigid (plunger-type with coil springs optional)
Rear Brake:	Drum
Weight:	245 pounds
Final Drive:	Chain
Owner:	Pete Bollenbach

Far left: *Though a plunger-type rear suspension was optional, Arrows came standard with a rigid frame, so the sprung saddle was a welcome feature. Below the saddle sits the horn, which was later moved to a more logical position at the front of the bike.* Left: *Chiefs had the speedometer mounted on the tank; the Arrow followed European practice and mounted it ahead of the handlebars. Note arrow pointer.* Below: *Since the Arrow was aimed at beginning riders, the gear indicator was a nice touch.*

1949 INDIAN SUPER SCOUT

When the Scout name reappeared on a line of 440cc (26-cubic-inch) vertical twins in 1949, many Indian aficionados felt the association inappropriate. As a result, in mid-1950 the engine was enlarged to 500cc (30.5 cubic inches) and the bike renamed the Warrior.

For what was essentially its only year of production (a few leftover '49s were sold as 1950 models), the Scout was offered in three versions. Base Scouts were stripped down to the bare essentials; Sport Scouts got a rearview mirror, center stand, front crash bar, and rear luggage rack; and Super Scouts added a windshield, dual spotlights, rear crash bars, and saddlebags.

Conceived in response to the ever-increasing postwar sales of foreign middleweight motorcycles, most notably Triumphs, the Scout (along with its single-cylinder linemate, the Arrow) featured more modern design principles than previous Indians. Tops among these were the switch to overhead-valve engines and adoption of foot shift. Other contemporary touches included telescopic forks, bench seat, and "thin" fenders.

In order to concentrate on these newcomers, Indian forestalled production of the mainstream Chief during 1949. Unfortunately, the verticals experienced numerous teething problems, and the combination didn't do struggling Indian any good. Nevertheless, the verticals are stylish machines that in many ways compare favorably to similar efforts of two decades later.

Year:	1949
Manufacturer:	Indian
Model:	Super Scout
Engine Type:	Vertical twin
Displacement:	26.6 cubic inches
Valve Train:	Overhead valves
Carburetion:	NA
Transmission:	Four-speed, foot shift
Front Suspension:	Hydraulic
Front Brake(s):	Drum
Rear Suspension:	Rigid (plunger-type with coil springs available)
Rear Brake:	Drum
Weight:	280 pounds
Final Drive:	Chain

Opposite page: *Some of the accessories that were standard on Super Scouts have been removed from this example, such as the windshield, dual spotlights, crash bars, and saddlebags.* This page, top left: *Warrior's 26.6-cubic-inch (440cc) vertical twin carried overhead valves—something new for Indian. Output is estimated at 20 horsepower.* Top right: *Scout's foot shift was on the left with down for low, just like modern bikes. Gear indicator is a nice touch. Left-side kickstarter, however, was awkward for most riders.* Left: *Early postwar verticals had unusual cross-two-spoke wheels, which proved weak; they were later updated to normal cross-four-spoke wheels as shown here.*

1951 INDIAN WARRIOR

Indian began building postwar "vertical" models in 1948: the Arrow, with a 13-cubic-inch single, and the Scout, with a 26-cubic-inch twin. Both deviated from the Indian norm by having modern hand-operated clutches, foot-actuated gearshifts, and hydraulic forks. But rear suspensions followed Indian tradition: a choice of rigid or plunger-type with coil springs.

To better compete with the 500cc (30-cubic-inch) Triumphs that were gaining in popularity, the Scout engine was enlarged to 30.4 cubic inches in 1950, and the motorcycle was renamed the Warrior.

Though Warrior production only lasted through 1952, several refinements were instituted along the way. Beginning in 1950, the gearbox was secured to the frame in order to reduce vibrations that were causing premature transmission failures. Also that year, the cross-two-spoke wheels were replaced by stronger cross-four-spoke wheels as on other Indians, and an adjustment mechanism was added for the primary chain.

Still more changes occurred for 1951, though the motorcycles themselves were mostly carryovers from the year before. Flashier paint schemes were the most obvious departure, but dealers were also provided with special kits to modify the ignition systems.

None of this, however, was enough to save foundering Indian. After production of the verticals ceased in 1952, the Chief V-twin labored on for one more year before Indian closed its doors forever.

Year:	1951
Manufacturer:	Indian
Model:	Warrior
Engine Type:	Vertical twin
Displacement:	30.4 cubic inches
Valve Train:	Overhead valves
Carburetion:	Amal
Transmission:	Four-speed, foot shift
Front Suspension:	Hydraulic
Front Brake(s):	Drum
Rear Suspension:	Plunger-type with coil springs
Rear Brake:	Drum
Weight:	315 pounds
Final Drive:	Chain
Owner:	Pete Bollenbach

Left: *To more directly compete with European bikes in the 500cc class, the 26.6-cubic-inch (436cc) Scout twin was bored out to 30.4 cubic inches (498cc) for the Warrior. Tank graphics were new for 1951.* Below: *Like the smaller Arrow, the Warrior had its speedometer mounted ahead of the handlebars, but added amp and oil-pressure gauges in a chrome housing.*

1952 HARLEY-DAVIDSON FL

After introducing the "Panhead" engine in 1948, Harley-Davidson added chrome-plated piston rings in 1952 to reduce wear and enhance durability. Though the Panhead was originally offered in two sizes, 61 and 74 cubic inches, the 74 so overshadowed its smaller sibling that the 61 was dropped after 1952.

Bigger news for '52 came in the form of a new hand clutch/foot shift arrangement, though the former hand shift/foot clutch was offered to traditionalists as an option. Also that year, wider fuel tanks with increased capacity were introduced. FLs gained modern "Hydra-Glide" hydraulic forks in 1949, but still employed a rigid frame lacking rear suspension.

It was during this period that motorcycling began to get some bad publicity, and despite Indian's impending demise, Harley sales dropped from 1948's record high of 31,000 to just over 17,000 in 1952—and even that number was not reached again until the mid-Sixties.

Year:	1952
Manufacturer:	Harley-Davidson
Model:	FL
Engine Type:	V-twin
Displacement:	74 cubic inches
Valve Train:	Overhead valves
Carburetion:	Schebler
Transmission:	Four-speed, foot shift (hand shift optional)
Front Suspension:	Hydraulic
Front Brake(s):	Drum
Rear Suspension:	Rigid
Rear Brake:	Drum
Weight:	560 pounds
Final Drive:	Chain
Owner:	John Archacki

Above: *Though this example is fitted with the new-for-'52 foot-shift transmission, the traditional hand shift was still offered as an option.* Left: *With the addition of hydraulic front forks for 1949, the big FL series became known as the Hydra-Glide. By 1952, they boasted a fancy chrome bezel surrounding the headlight and upper fork tubes.* Lower left: *Simple chrome tank trim gives the 1952 Hydra Glide a stately appearance.* Below: *After 1952, all "Panheads" displaced 74 cubic inches—the 61 cubic-inch version was dropped due to lack of interest.*

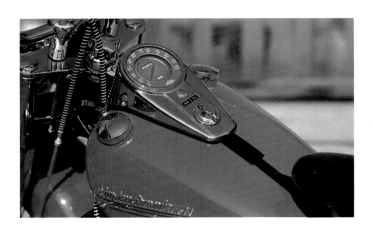

1953 INDIAN CHIEF

By 1953, the sole surviving Indian was the V-twin Chief, which had received continual updating since the war. Its leaf-spring front suspension was replaced by a girder-style front end in 1946, which in turn gave way to modern hydraulic forks in 1950. Also that year, the Chief's flathead V-twin was enlarged from 74 to 80 cubic inches, and foot shift was introduced, though the latter didn't become a regular production feature until 1951.

For 1952, the traditional sprung saddle was replaced by a solid-mounted seat, and protective cowling appeared over the distributor. Other changes showed up in swan-song '53. The transmission was now lubricated separately from the primary drive, and the headlight high/low-beam switch was moved from the handlebar to the left-side running board.

Though the Chief's flathead V-twin was considered somewhat archaic compared to Harley-Davidson's overhead-valve engines, the Indian had a more modern ignition system. Whereas Harley used a single coil that fired both plugs at the same time once per revolution (one plug firing needlessly), Indian used an automotive-type distributor that fired each plug only on its cylinder's power stroke. This was hardly an overwhelming advantage, however, and Indian finally succumbed to Harley-Davidson and a wartime economy.

With its massive skirted fenders, locomotive-like torque, and "last-of-the-breed" heritage, the '53 Chief is surely one of the most collectible of Indians. It represents both the crowning achievement and the sorrowful end of a company that gave generations of motorcyclists some of their fondest memories.

Year:	1953
Manufacturer:	Indian
Model:	Chief
Engine Type:	V-twin
Displacement:	80 cubic inches
Valve Train:	Side valves
Carburetion:	Amal
Transmission:	Three-speed, hand shift
Front Suspension:	Hydraulic
Front Brake(s):	Drum
Rear Suspension:	Plunger-type with coil springs
Rear Brake:	Drum
Weight:	570 pounds
Final Drive:	Chain

Opposite page and above: *The '53 Chief carried acres of sheetmetal bodywork—and the tangerine example shown is lacking the available engine cowl that would fit between the exhaust-pipe downtubes.* Left: *Tank was awash with chrome trim. Note Indian-head shift knob.* Lower left: *By this time, Harley-Davidson was offering a modern foot-shift transmission, but Indian kept the old hand-shift with its foot-actuated clutch. Button on running board is the headlight high/low switch, moved there in '53, the Chief's final year.* Below: *"Full-dress" Chief with windshield, tool kit, engine cowl, seat fringe, and saddle bags—all popular accessories of the day.*

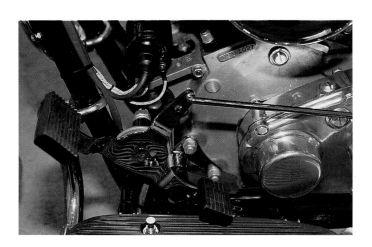

1954 HARLEY-DAVIDSON FLF

As the curtain rose for the 1954 model year, Harley-Davidson stood alone as the sole surviving American motorcycle manufacturer. Indian had folded its tent at the end of 1953, and all other U.S. manufacturers had vanished long before.

But the demise of Indian didn't mean that Harley-Davidson had no competition. There were a host of foreign manufacturers trying to gain a foothold in the lucrative U.S. market, and though most concentrated on smaller-displacement machines, some, like Triumph, vied for Harley's traditional customers.

Nineteen fifty-three marked Harley-Davidson's 50th Anniversary, and the company created a special medallion to commemorate the occasion. Strangely enough, the medallion didn't appear on the 1953 models, but rather on the '54s, mounted atop the front fender.

Also evident in 1954 were fuel tanks and fenders painted in contrasting colors. Two-toning was common on automobiles of the era, and Harley decided to try it too. While the practice continued for some time, it was soon altered so that each body piece carried the same two-tone paint scheme. Starting in 1952, FLs were offered with either hand or foot shift, the latter (shown here) being designated FLF.

Year:	1954
Manufacturer:	Harley-Davidson
Model:	FLF
Engine Type:	V-twin
Displacement:	74 cubic inches
Valve Train:	Overhead valves
Carburetion:	Schebler
Transmission:	Four-speed, foot shift (hand shift optional)
Front Suspension:	Hydraulic
Front Brake(s):	Drum
Rear Suspension:	Rigid
Rear Brake:	Drum
Weight:	560 pounds
Final Drive:	Chain
Owner:	Dale Walksler Collection

Opposite page: *Dual spotlights were a popular accessory of the time, adding greatly to nighttime visibility.* This page, top: *FLs came with the old hand shift, while FLFs, like the example shown, had foot shift.* Left: *Big Harleys continued with the traditional tank-mounted speedometer.* Above: *Front fender advertised the FLF's overhead-valve V-twin—though any enthusiast worth his salt already knew.*

1957 HARLEY-DAVIDSON FLH

Harley-Davidson's big news for 1957 was the introduction of the Sportster, a 55-cubic-inch V-twin with true "sporting" properties—at least when compared to the company's mainstream machines like the FLH.

Though the Sportster was quite modern for its time, the large Harleys remained mired in tradition. A foot shift was available, yet many were sold with the old-fashioned "suicide" hand shift. It would also be the last big Harley to ride a rigid frame offering no rear suspension. The "Panhead" engine that arrived in 1948 bore few changes, still displacing 74 cubic inches.

A redesigned tank badge marked the large Harleys for '57, but little else was new. Offerings included the FL and FLH, the latter being pictured here. The "H" stood for "Highway," and those models offered some added features over the FLs. But the major significance to collectors is that only 164 FLHs were built that year out of Harley's total production of over 13,000 motorcycles.

Year:	1957
Manufacturer:	Harley-Davidson
Model:	FLH
Engine Type:	V-twin
Displacement:	74 cubic inches
Valve Train:	Overhead valves
Carburetion:	Linkert
Transmission:	Four-speed, foot shift (hand shift optional)
Front Suspension:	Hydraulic
Front Brake(s):	Drum
Rear Suspension:	Rigid
Rear Brake:	Drum
Weight:	NA
Final Drive:	Chain
Owner:	William P. Dokianos

Above: *FLHs were so rare (only 164 built in 1957) because they had the top-line "Highway" accessories, but the old hand-shift transmission with foot clutch. With foot shift, the model became the FLHF, of which more than 2600 were built. Left: Tank trim changed almost yearly during this period, but the trusty "Panhead" V-twin would carry on until the mid-'60s. Opposite page: Large saddle had a spring-loaded seat post along with rear "helper springs" that could be swung up into position when more support was required.*

1960 HARLEY-DAVIDSON FLHF

Harley-Davidson enthusiasts enjoyed another quantum leap in ride comfort when the company added a modern swingarm rear suspension system to the FLs in 1958. Called the Duo-Glide, this model continued for several years with only minor changes. In '59 it wore a more aggressive arrow logo, and for 1960, a new headlight housing was adopted that added a sleeker look. Dual spotlights, seen on the '60 model pictured, were a popular option during that time that greatly improved nighttime safety.

As before, both foot- and hand-shift versions of the FLs were offered, the former adding an "F" suffix. Despite having rear suspension, the '60 Duo-Glides featured a spring-loaded saddle post for added comfort. The FLHF shown sports the optional 2-into-2 exhaust system.

Nearly 6000 FLs were built in 1960, when Harley's sales jumped 16 percent. Part of the company's success was no doubt due to its showing at the Daytona races that year, as Harley-mounted riders swept the events.

Year:	1960
Manufacturer:	Harley-Davidson
Model:	FLHF
Engine Type:	V-twin
Displacement:	74 cubic inches
Valve Train:	Overhead valves
Carburetion:	Schebler
Transmission:	Four-speed, foot shift (hand shift optional)
Front Suspension:	Hydraulic
Front Brake(s):	Drum
Rear Suspension:	Swingarm with coil-over shocks
Rear Brake:	Drum
Weight:	560 pounds
Final Drive:	Chain
Owner:	John Archacki

Top: *With the Duo-Glide of 1958 came a swingarm rear suspension with coil-over shocks to (finally) replace the rigid frame. Nonetheless, the model retained a sprung saddle to add an extra margin of comfort.* Left: *Power still came from the reliable 74-cubic-inch "Panhead" V-twin, as it had since '48.* Above: *Speedometer graphics were changed, nicely matching this example's metallic green paint.*

1965 HARLEY-DAVIDSON FL ELECTRA GLIDE

For Harley-Davidson, 1965 marked the end of an era. The Electra Glide, with its electric starter, made its debut, but it would be the last year for the famous "Panhead" engine that was introduced in 1948.

That engine had received some modifications over the years, a significant one coming in 1963 with external oil lines that improved lubrication to the cylinder heads. As a result, the '63-'65 FL models are highly sought-after by collectors—the '65s most of all, because of their electric starter. A large battery case on the right side makes the Electra Glide easily distinguishable from earlier FLs.

The Electra Glide pictured is equipped with the dual-muffler exhaust system that was optional on big Harleys during this era (as was the old hand shift with foot clutch). Exhaust from the front cylinder exited to the right, while that from the rear cylinder exited to the left, both terminating in their own distinctive "fishtail" muffler. Standard was the usual system that had both cylinders exhausting to the right into a single muffler.

Though a curb weight of more than 700 pounds restricts performance somewhat, the Electra Glide remains a popular motorcycle, not only to collectors but also to those intent on using them as daily transportation. With the addition of electric starting, they provide most of the features of a modern touring bike, making long trips very comfortable indeed.

Year:	1965
Manufacturer:	Harley-Davidson
Model:	FL Electra Glide
Engine Type:	V-twin
Displacement:	74 cubic inches
Valve Train:	Overhead valves
Carburetion:	Bendix
Transmission:	Four-speed, foot shift (hand shift optional)
Front Suspension:	Hydraulic
Front Brake(s):	Drum
Rear Suspension:	Swingarm with coil-over shocks
Rear Brake:	Drum
Weight:	783 pounds
Final Drive:	Chain

Far left: *Mammoth chrome headlight bezel first appeared in 1960.* Above: *Electra Glide script on front fender advertised the new electric starter introduced in 1965.* Left: *Starter was mounted at the forward end of the crankcase, between the front cylinder and exhaust pipe. Nineteen sixty-five would be the last year for the "Panhead" engine, introduced in 1948.*

1965 HARLEY-DAVIDSON SPORTSTER

Few motorcycles have had the impact of the Harley Sportster, introduced in 1957. With its 54-cubic-inch overhead-valve V-twin, four-speed foot-shift transmission, and modern front and rear suspension, the Sportster would eventually eclipse the bigger FL models in sales.

Designated the XL series, the first Sportsters were essentially updated versions of the 45-cubic-inch (later 55-cubic-inch) flathead K models built between 1952 and 1956. With the new overhead-valve engine came four (yes, *four*) separate camshafts, each operating its own valve. Unlike the larger 74-cubic-inch Harleys, the Sportster's engine and transmission were integrated into one unit, rather than having separate cases. Otherwise, the Sportster continued with the same chassis and running gear as the K.

In its second year, the Sportster gained higher compression and larger valves, with higher-lift cams coming in 1959. Also added was the XLCH, an even sportier Sportster with high pipes, "peanut" gas tank, and other alterations.

A switch from 6-volt to 12-volt electrics occurred in 1965, when the bike pictured was built. Though electric start was still two years away for the Sportster, the bigger FLs got it in 1965, and Harley used the same generator for all its motorcycles. Many other changes were to come, and though the bike is still with us today, many feel these early models to be the best of the bunch.

Year:	1965
Manufacturer:	Harley-Davidson
Model:	XLCH
Engine Type:	V-twin
Displacement:	54 cubic inches
Valve Train:	Overhead valves
Carburetion:	Bendix
Transmission:	Four-speed, foot shift
Front Suspension:	Hydraulic
Front Brake(s):	Drum
Rear Suspension:	Swingarm with coil-over shocks
Rear Brake:	Drum
Weight:	480 pounds
Final Drive:	Chain
Owner:	Tom Scott

Top: *Sportster engines were built in unit with the transmission, while the bigger Harleys had (and continue to have) a separate engine and transmission.* Left: *The XLCH's headlight hood and fork brace became Harley signatures, later to be used on "custom" versions of the company's bigger bikes.*

1971 HARLEY-DAVIDSON BAJA 100

When most people think of Harley-Davidson, the image of a rumbling V-twin springs instantly to mind. But since World War II, the company has offered small two-strokes, scooters, snowmobiles, and even golf carts.

Harley's first postwar foray into the "entry-level" market occurred a year after production resumed. A little 125cc two-stroke single was introduced for 1948 in an effort to draw young riders into Harley-Davidson showrooms. This machine grew to 165cc and later 175cc, and was joined by a scooter called the Topper in 1959. Added in 1961 was a 250cc (later 350cc) four-stroke single produced by an Italian firm called Aermacchi, of whom Harley had purchased a half interest. Other machines as small as 50cc were offered starting in the mid-1960s.

In 1970, the Baja 100 debuted. A stripped-down dirt bike, the Baja was powered by a 98cc (6-cubic-inch) high-performance two-stroke single. With a short 52-inch wheelbase, loads of ground clearance, and knobby tires, it proved fairly successful in various off-road racing events, and even won the legendary Greenhorn Enduro.

Officially designated the MSR-100 (and later the SR-100), it was built for five years before being discontinued, production never exceeding 1500 units in any year. A lighting option was offered in 1972 and an automatic gas-oil mixing system added in '73, but neither were enough to save it from the inevitable onslaught of cheap, high-tech Japanese imports.

Year:	1971
Manufacturer:	Harley-Davidson
Model:	Baja 100
Engine Type:	Single-cylinder
Displacement:	98cc
Valve Train:	Two-stroke
Carburetion:	NA
Transmission:	Five-speed, foot shift
Front Suspension:	Hydraulic
Front Brake(s):	Drum
Rear Suspension:	Swingarm with coil-over shocks
Rear Brake:	Drum
Weight:	NA
Final Drive:	Chain
Owner:	Illinois Harley-Davidson

Top: *Though fairly successful in competition, the Baja 100 just wasn't the type of motorcycle Harley-Davidson was known for, and sales never met expectations.* Left: *Spunky little two-stroke single sported huge cooling fins; piston itself was less than two inches in diameter.* Above: *Fuel tank was topped with a matte-black panel. Hose at front is an overflow so that fuel wouldn't spill on the hot cylinder.*

1971 HARLEY-DAVIDSON XLH SPORTSTER

One of Harley-Davidson's first attempts at factory customizing took the form of a fiberglass tail section for the 1970 Sportster. Patterned after Cafe-Racer bodywork of the period, the design spawned a similar tailpiece that graced the first of the famed Super Glides in 1971. Conceived by William "Willie G" Davidson, the stylish sculpture continued as a $60 option on the '71 Sportster, but disappeared after that due to buyer indifference.

Harley-Davidson stressed the custom theme even further in 1971 by offering a variety of optional equipment and color combinations for the Sportster. The most collectible of these turned out to be the "Sparkling America" paint scheme, a $40 option that clothed your Sportster in good ol' red, white, and blue. The Sparkling Turquoise on the bike pictured was another optional color, this one priced at about $7.

Though short-lived, this design proved that Harley-Davidson was willing to adventure out on a styling limb to bring its customers something different—a philosophy that carries on to this day.

Year:	1971
Manufacturer:	Harley-Davidson
Model:	XLH
Engine Type:	V-twin
Displacement:	54 cubic inches
Valve Train:	Overhead valves
Carburetion:	Schebler
Transmission:	Four-speed, foot shift
Front Suspension:	Hydraulic
Front Brake(s):	Drum
Rear Suspension:	Swingarm with coil-over shocks
Rear Brake:	Drum
Weight:	508 pounds
Final Drive:	Chain
Owner:	Buzz Walneck

Left and opposite page: *Fiberglass tail debuted as standard equipment on 1970 Sportsters, but proved unpopular. It was made optional in 1971. Far left: This instrument panel would face Sportster riders for some time to come. Below: Right-side shift would switch to the left side in '72 per government mandate.*

1975 HARLEY-DAVIDSON XR-750

Introduced in 1970, the XR-750 was a purpose-built racing bike aimed at dirt-track competition. As such, it lacked equipment necessary to make it streetable, such as turn signals, lights, starter (not even a kickstarter), horn, mufflers, and (at least on early models) brakes.

In its first two years of production, the XR came with iron cylinders and heads, which proved to be a weak link. Alloy cylinders and heads were substituted in 1972, and performance improved tremendously. Maximum compression with the iron components was 8:1; the alloy parts allowed ratios as high as 10.5:1, adding about 20 horsepower. It also gained a rear disc brake.

Early XR-750s carried straight silver exhaust pipes that exited low on the right side. Later models had black pipes with megaphone mufflers that exited high on the left, such as the '75 model pictured here. Harley aficionados will notice that the rear cylinder head of the 750cc (45-cubic-inch) V-twin is configured so that the exhaust valve faces the front rather than the rear as was the practice in the company's street machines of the day.

Weighing in at less than 300 pounds and boasting a claimed 90 horsepower, the XR-750 was all business. The throttle went from idle to wide open in only one-quarter turn—essentially a 90-horsepower light switch.

For more than a decade, the XR-750 tore up the dirt tracks, and even made its mark on some road-racing courses. It took an onslaught of Japan's best to eventually unseat it as the reigning King of the Dirt.

Year:	1975
Manufacturer:	Harley-Davidson
Model:	XR-750
Engine Type:	V-twin
Displacement:	45 cubic inches
Valve Train:	Overhead valves
Carburetion:	Dual Mikuni
Transmission:	Four-speed, foot shift
Front Suspension:	Hydraulic
Front Brake(s):	None
Rear Suspension:	Swingarm with coil-over shocks
Rear Brake:	Disc
Weight:	290 pounds
Final Drive:	Chain
Owner:	Dale Walksler Collection

Left: *Later versions of the XR-750 gained a rear disc brake and aluminum cylinder heads. With the new heads came exhaust pipes that were rerouted so that they exited to the left side of the bike rather than to the right as before.* Below: *Dual Mikuni carburetors were also used on aluminum-head versions.*

1977 HARLEY-DAVIDSON XLCR

By 1977, Harley-Davidson was used to taking styling risks. The "boat-tailed" Sportster of 1970 and similar Super Glide of '71 heralded an era of factory-customized motorcycles that continues to this day.

Though some of Harley's styling exercises were not commercial successes when new, most eventually became valued collector's items. None illustrate that point better than the '77 XLCR pictured here.

Known more for its chopper-style customs than its road-racing prowess, Harley's XLCR Cafe Racer didn't appeal to the company's typical clientele. And despite carrying the most powerful production engine Harley had ever built, the XLCR really wasn't in the same league as the imported "crotch rockets" of the day, so neither was it about to make many conquest sales based on its performance.

As a result, the bikes languished on showroom floors. Available again for 1978, dealers offered big discounts to move them out the door. But in an almost expected turn of events, the XLCR is now a coveted classic bringing top dollar on the collector market.

Year:	1977
Manufacturer:	Harley-Davidson
Model:	XLCR
Engine Type:	V-twin
Displacement:	61 cubic inches
Valve Train:	Overhead valves
Carburetion:	NA
Transmission:	Four-speed, foot shift
Front Suspension:	Hydraulic
Front Brake(s):	Dual disc
Rear Suspension:	Swingarm with coil-over shocks
Rear Brake:	Disc
Weight:	485 pounds
Final Drive:	Chain
Owner:	Estate of Garth Ware

Opposite page and this page, top: *With its handlebar fairing, streamlined tail section, angular tank, chromeless profile, alloy wheels, and stiff suspension, the XLCR just wasn't going in the same direction most Harley enthusiasts were heading. As a result, it wasn't very popular when it was new—though that would later change. Left: The XLCR's 61-cubic-inch (1000cc) V-twin received several performance tweaks, making it the most powerful street engine Harley had ever offered. Note siamesed exhaust headers that split into separate pipes.*

1981 HARLEY-DAVIDSON HERITAGE EDITION

Harley-Davidson celebrated its 75th Anniversary in 1978, and one of the product highlights of that year was the return of an 80-cubic-inch V-twin, absent from the line since World War II. Soon afterward, the "retro" look came into vogue at Harley-Davidson, a styling trend that continues to this day. One of the first products to combine these two features was the 1981 Heritage Edition.

Carrying a two-place saddle, headlight nacelle, green and orange paint, and other features seen on classic Harleys of yesteryear (but equipped with modern suspension and brakes), only 784 Heritage Editions were built for 1981, and the model did not return in '82. With its time-honored styling and low production numbers, the Heritage itself has now become a coveted classic.

But perhaps overshadowing any of Harley-Davidson's product offerings in 1981 was a much larger event that took place in June of that year. After more than a decade under the AMF banner, a group of Harley-Davidson employees arranged financing and bought back the company. While production and profits both increased under AMF, quality didn't. After the buy-out, employees and enthusiasts alike took a new pride in Harley-Davidson.

Year:	1981
Manufacturer:	Harley-Davidson
Model:	Heritage Edition
Engine Type:	V-twin
Displacement:	80 cubic inches
Valve Train:	Overhead valves
Carburetion:	NA
Transmission:	Four-speed, foot shift
Front Suspension:	Hydraulic
Front Brake(s):	Disc
Rear Suspension:	Swingarm with coil-over shock
Rear Brake:	Disc
Weight:	NA
Final Drive:	Chain
Owner:	Jim Kersting Family Collection

Top left: *For those who might wonder what to call the green and orange dresser, the front fender spelled it out for them.* Left: *A Heritage Edition emblem also graced the primary cover.* Above: *By this time, Harley had moved the choke knob to a more convenient location on the instrument panel, where the owner's name could be engraved on a special Heritage Edition plaque.*

1988 HARLEY-DAVIDSON FXSTS SOFTAIL SPRINGER

Yet another example of Harley-Davidson combining classic and modern styling elements can be seen in the 1988 FXSTS Softail Springer. The Springer front end, designed after those used before Hydra-Glide hydraulic forks debuted in 1949, employs a leading-link design activating compression and rebound springs (joined now by a modern hydraulic shock). In back, the Softail suspension gives the look of being a rigid frame, but instead pivots like a swingarm, compressing a pair of coil-over shocks hidden beneath the seat.

Back in 1980, Harley had resurrected another idea from its past: belt drive. First appearing on a new Sturgis model, belts were used for both the primary drive (connecting the engine to the transmission) and secondary drive (transmission to rear wheel). Of course, they weren't leather belts as used in the early years, but rather toothed rubber belts with reinforcing strands. Lighter and quieter than chains, they required no lubrication. Compared to shaft drive, they were cheaper and didn't invoke "pogoing" effects during throttle transitions. As a result, belt drive would prove to be a popular feature of many Harleys to come.

One of those was this 1988 Softail Springer, one of three models selected during Harley-Davidson's 85th Anniversary year to wear special paint and badges commemorating the event.

Year:	1988
Manufacturer:	Harley-Davidson
Model:	FXSTS
Engine Type:	V-twin
Displacement:	80 cubic inches
Valve Train:	Overhead valves
Carburetion:	Schebler
Transmission:	Five-speed, foot shift
Front Suspension:	Leading link with coil springs and hydraulic shock
Front Brake(s):	Disc
Rear Suspension:	Triangulated swingarm with coil-over shock
Rear Brake:	Disc
Weight:	NA
Final Drive:	Belt
Owner:	Lake Shore Harley-Davidson

Top: "Softail" rear suspension incorporates a triangulated swingarm that pivots at the bottom and compresses a pair of coil-over shocks underneath the seat. Left: Springer front fork is similar to those offered by Harley-Davidson prior to 1949, though it adds a shock absorber to improve control. Above: Gas caps wear 85th Anniversary emblems, while similar decals grace the front fender and side of the fuel tank.

1993 HARLEY-DAVIDSON FXDWG

As with previous anniversaries, Harley-Davidson's 90th was celebrated with specially designed and badged models. This time around, it was the Wide Glide that got the treatment.

First introduced in 1980, the Wide Glide featured a flamed "Fat Bob" gas tank, narrow front wheel, "ape hanger" handlebars, forward-mounted foot pegs, and bobbed rear fender. That look carried through to the 90th Anniversary Edition, though a two-tone silver paint scheme replaced the 1980 model's flames.

Beneath the custom styling rests the usual Harley mechanicals, including modern suspension, disc brakes, and of course, the thumping 80-cubic-inch V-twin. Unlike the original, however, the 90th Anniversary Edition boasts silent-running, maintenance-free belt drive.

To those familiar with the company's history, the mere presence of a 90th Anniversary Harley-Davidson was a cause for celebration. Several times over the years the Milwaukee company looked as though it was on the verge of extinction, most recently in the early 1980s. But by constantly improving styling and engineering—and keeping in close contact with its clientele—Harley found itself celebrating its 90th birthday in the enviable position of not being able to keep up with orders. No doubt the FXDWG only added to that problem.

Year:	1993
Manufacturer:	Harley-Davidson
Model:	FXDWG
Engine Type:	V-twin
Displacement:	80 cubic inches
Valve Train:	Overhead valves
Carburetion:	NA
Transmission:	Five-speed, foot shift
Front Suspension:	Hydraulic
Front Brake(s):	Disc
Rear Suspension:	Swingarm with coil-over shocks
Rear Brake:	Disc
Weight:	598 pounds
Final Drive:	Belt
Owner:	Lee Mattes

Left and above: *Like previous anniversary editions, the 90th Anniversary Wide Glide boasted several commemorative emblems. Below: Wide Glides got their name from the wide spacing between their extended front fork tubes.*

1993 HARLEY-DAVIDSON FLSTN

Ever since William "Willie G." Davidson, grandson of a Harley-Davidson founder, took over as chief of design in 1963, the company has shown a willingness—a passion even—for bringing daring designs to market. But this one is unusual even by Harley-Davidson standards.

For 1993, Harley offered its usual anniversary models to celebrate the company's 90th birthday. And right alongside those two-tone silver bikes was this striking black-and-white model with heifer trim, soon to be nicknamed the "Cow Glide."

Combining the classic look of wire wheels, whitewall tires, running boards, and chromed headlight nacelle with the black-on-white paint scheme results in a stunning appearance. Add the bovine trim, and the image is truly unique.

But like other Harley-Davidson "factory customs," the FLSTN boasts modern mechanicals, such as belt drive, disc brakes, hydraulic forks, and Harley's Softail frame that looks rigid, but isn't. Also like most of its other customs, the Cow Glide sold out immediately, its 2700 copies sure to be collector's items one day.

Year:	1993
Manufacturer:	Harley-Davidson
Model:	FLSTN
Engine Type:	V-twin
Displacement:	80 cubic inches
Valve Train:	Overhead valves
Carburetion:	Schebler
Transmission:	Five-speed with foot shift
Front Suspension:	Hydraulic
Front Brake(s):	Disc
Rear Suspension:	Triangulated swing-arm with coil-over shocks
Rear Brake:	Disc
Weight:	710 pounds
Final Drive:	Belt
Owner:	Claudio Rauzi

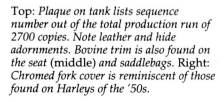

Top: Plaque on tank lists sequence number out of the total production run of 2700 copies. Note leather and hide adornments. Bovine trim is also found on the seat (middle) and saddlebags. Right: Chromed fork cover is reminiscent of those found on Harleys of the '50s.

1994 HARLEY-DAVIDSON FLHTC ULTRA

Ever since motorcycles took to the streets, riders have enjoyed the wind rushing through their hair. As speeds and travel distances increased, however, some didn't enjoy it as much.

It wasn't until the 1940s that windshields became common, the military being among the first to use them—with the hope of stopping more than just wind from going through the rider's hair. Later in the decade, Harley-Davidson offered a roll-up windshield as an option on civilian bikes.

In those days, riders felt lucky to get instruments and warning lights on their mounts. As might be expected, motorcycling has come a long way since then. The FLHTC Ultra features air-adjustable suspension, quiet belt-drive, an electronic cruise control, CB radio, AM/FM amplified stereo with weather band that includes remote controls for the passenger, a spacious rear trunk, and heavily-padded seats with backrests, all of which make its passengers feel right at home—even when they're miles away.

In the old days, riders probably never dreamed that touring could be so luxurious. Nowadays they don't have to.

Year:	1994
Manufacturer:	Harley-Davidson
Model:	FLHTC Ultra
Engine Type:	V-twin
Displacement:	80 cubic inches
Valve Train:	Overhead valves
Carburetion:	Schebler
Transmission:	Five-speed, foot shift
Front Suspension:	Air-adjustable hydraulic
Front Brake(s):	Dual discs
Rear Suspension:	Swingarm with air-adjustable coil-over shocks
Rear Brake:	Disc
Weight:	765 pounds
Final Drive:	Belt
Owner:	Heritage Harley-Davidson

Far left: *Lower fairing incorporates some added storage space.* Left: *A throne fit for a King—and Queen. Note stereo speakers.* Above: *Script on front fender says it all.*

INDEX